People | Food | Culture

Delicious

MYANMAR

Discover Myanmar through its People and Food

Juan Gallardo

ISBN-13: 978-1-941142-33-2
ISBN-10: 1941142338

Editor: Deidre Forbes
Designer: Debbie O'Byrne
Photographer: Juan Gallardo

www.deliciousmyanmar.com

I want to thank everyone in this book for welcoming me into their homes and teaching me about authentic Burmese cuisine, for guiding me around Myanmar and making me feel so at home.

I also want to thank my family and friends for supporting me throughout this adventure.

Myanmar

100 km

100 miles

JUAN GALLARDO

INTRODUCTION

It was my passion for Southeast Asia, fuelled by my curiosity about a country closed to tourists for so many years, that brought me, my backpack and my camera to Myanmar in January 2014.

Myanmar, or Burma as it was known until 1989 when the military government renamed it, is a fascinating country rich in culture, history, natural beauty and resources.

Here you can find almost all types of habitats, from the frozen alpine of the Himalayas in the north to steamy jungles, coral reefs and open grasslands. A third of its perimeter is unspoilt coastline along the Bay of Bengal and the Andaman Sea.

Despite the fact that the country is undergoing a rapid phase of modernisation – like no other country in Southeast Asia – it has noticeably retained much of its British colonial heritage.

This backdrop of colonial buildings, monks asking for alms, rickshaw taxis passing by, men wearing skirts (longyi) and women with thanaka on their faces combine to create a truly surreal setting.

It is the picture perfect location in the heart of Asia! But it gets better. With an ethnically diverse population of 135 different recognised groups and many different religions, the majority (80%) being Buddhists, it is the people who make a real difference in Myanmar.

A proud people, they leave a lasting impression. They will touch your heart with their warmth and sincerity, their kindness and generosity. I travelled all over the country, meeting locals and finding out first-hand about their culture, customs and cuisine and it was this amazing experience that inspired this book. And after discovering how delicious and varied their food was, I was determined to learn all about it and share it with you.

Myanmar borders Laos, Thailand, China, Bangladesh and India and has been strongly influenced by its powerful neighbours, not only in culture, art and religion, but also in cuisine. If Asian food is one of the best and most varied in the world, imagine a country with its own delicious cuisine plus a healthy dose of Asian ingredients and cooking styles – including

Chinese bean curd and soya sauce, the curries and spices of India, and from Thailand a taste for snacking on fried insects!

Burmese cuisine is also extremely healthy, favouring fresh fruit and vegetables, as well as fish products like fish sauce and fish paste and fermented seafood. The locals love mangoes, and pork is the preferred meat while lahpet (pickled tea leaf) is the leaf of choice.

Traditionally meals are served on a low, round table, small enough for everyone to reach all the dishes. Diners sit on the floor or on a mat. The elderly and guests are given priority, and they eat with their right hand. Chopsticks and Chinese style spoons are used for noodle soups, and for salads you can use either a spoon or a fork.

A typical meal includes a salad, a curry dish, a dried fish dish, a soup and fresh or boiled vegetables to dip in a salty fish paste sauce. All dishes are served at the same time with rice so you can choose and combine as you want. As for drinks, water and green tea are the most common options and at the end of the meal, jaggery is usually served.

With this book I will take you all over Myanmar and show you how to cook the most delicious dishes with the real masters of Burmese cuisine: the locals.

I will introduce you to interesting people from various religions, ethnic groups and social classes. Filled with the hospitality and generosity of the local families, *Delicious Myanmar* comes to you from *their* kitchens.

Fall in love with the beauty of Myanmar, the Golden Land, its people and their cuisine – as I did. Enjoy!

Juan Gallardo

JUAN GALLARDO

CONTENTS

34 Watercress Salad

36 Fish Balls with Tomato

38 Fish Curry

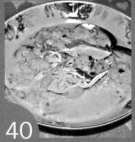

40 Shwe Yin Aye

42 Thanaka

44 Beena Shah

46 Paneer Makhani

48 Mix Dal Makhani

50 Shwedagon Pagoda

52 Gold Pounders Workshop

54 U Bein Bridge

56 Inwa (Or Ava)

58 Mingun

60 Coconut Noodles

62 Saing Oo

64 Potato, Egg and Tomato Curry

66 Tealeaf Salad

68 Papaya Curry

70 Pumpkin Curry

72 Sticky Rice and Music

74 Gokteik Viaduct

78 Shwan Ku, Padaung Ethnic Group Village

80 Sticky Rice Stuffed in Bamboo

82 Bamboo Buddha Monastery

84 Yin Yin Than

86 Sweet Chicken Curry with Tomato

88 Fish Paste with Green Pepper

90 Marian Fruit Salad

92 Fermented Soybean Paste Salad

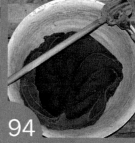

94 Fermented Soybean Paste Workshop

96 Bagan

98 Burmese Parasols

100 Bamboo Hat

102 Moe Zaw

104 Chilli Crab

106 Fish in Banana Leaf

108 Tiger Prawn Curry

110 Rakhine Fish Curry

112 Ngapali Beach

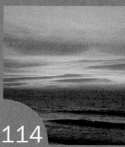

114 Ngwe Saung Beach

JUAN GALLARDO

DAW HINN SHWE

Daw Hinn Shwe is 70-years-old.

She lives in Dawei, the capital city of the Tanintharyi Region of Southeastern Myanmar. Her home is a traditional teak house with the kitchen underneath. She has lived here, with her family, all her life.

Her grandson Phyo learnt to cook whilst helping her lift heavy pots and pans in the kitchen. Phyo works in the Dawei Special Economic Zone where he is in charge of relocating people who live in the area where the new port will be built. Once this project is finished, he wants to work for a Non Governmental Organization (NGO) in Myanmar or Thailand.

FISH AND KIN-MON-CHIN YWAT (SOUR LEAF)

1. Cut the fish into slices. Add chicken powder and salt and mix together.
2. Heat oil and turmeric powder. Parcook the fish and put aside to debone.
3. Remove the leaves from the Kin-mon-chin pin (plant) and slice onions. Mix onions, leaves, oil, salt, chicken powder, rice powder and flour.
4. Add fish and mix again.
5. Wrap the mixture with plant leaves (banana or similar) and barbeque.

It is also possible to steam or fry (without the wrapping leaves). You can prepare this dish with any fish or seafood and it's also the same recipe for meat. Never change the Kin-mon-chin ywat, it's the main ingredient and gives the dish an amazing tangy flavour.

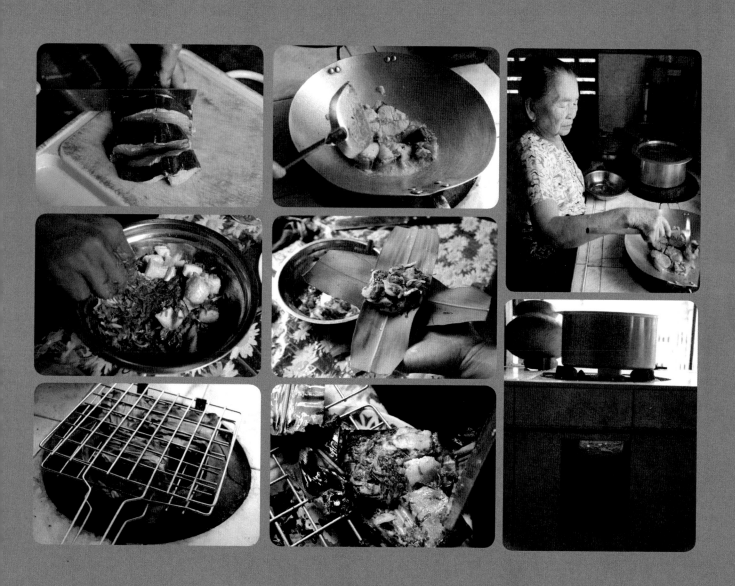

MAUNGMAGAN

Maungmagan is a beautiful beach and village located near Dawei, where villagers live on fishing activities.

The beach is popular with locals who usually go on Sundays and public holidays to enjoy time with family and friends.The majority of the locals wear normal clothes at the beach. Foreigners can wear swimming costumes but may attract some attention.

There are several beer stations and restaurants by the beach where you can either sit down and order food or bring your own food and use their space for a small cost.

It's a quiet beach with less tourists than other beaches in Myanmar.

NAN TO NGE

Nan To Nge is 63-years-old and lives in Hsipaw, Shan State.

She started selling Shan noodles in 1986, always using the same recipe which she learnt from her grandmother. Her family owns a noodle factory next to her house which supplies the noodles for her little tea shop (see page 12).

Her noodle dishes are just 300 kyats ($ 0.3) because Nan To Nge isn't interested in making money, she just wants to make people happy.

As a child, she lived next door to the palace where the Shan prince Sao Kya Seng lived and she often played with her royal neighbour.

One of her dreams… to visit England.

JUAN GALLARDO

SHAN NOODLES (SOUP AND SALAD)

Shan noodles are one of the most popular dishes in Myanmar – you'll find them in every teahouse and restaurant! You can have them either as a soup or as a salad, and in both cases the sauce is the same.

Tomato Sauce: blend tomatoes then add salt, sugar, oil, sugar cane sauce and paprika. Put in a pot and boil. When the colour changes, it's ready. The more time the better but keep adding water as necessary if it's very long time!

A big pot like the one Nan To Nge uses, takes four hours. For a small pot, 15 minutes should be ok.

SOUP: Boiling water, flat sticky rice noodle, tomato sauce, salt, sugar, sugar cane sauce, fermented soy bean powder, oil-garlic-turmeric sauce, spring onions and coriander (optional).

SALAD: Thick rice noodle, tomato sauce, salt, sugar, sugar cane sauce, cooked bean powder (Dah), oil-garlic-turmeric sauce, spring onions and coriander (optional).

JUAN GALLARDO

RICE NOODLE FACTORY

Nan To Nge's rice noodles factory in Hsipaw, Shan State.

Here they make rice noodles everyday and as you can see in the pictures, the process is mostly manual - from making the dough to actually determining the size and thickness of the noodle.

Just add Nan To Nge's sauce to the noodles and you'll want to keep coming back to Hsipaw for more!

BLACK SESAME SEED AND STICKY RICE CAKE (KHOR POAT) WORKSHOP AT HSIPAW, SHAN STATE

This is a very traditional snack in Shan State made with purple rice, black and round sesame seeds and salt.

Preparation: Place the cooked rice into a stone "bowl" situated in the ground and add black round sesame seeds (already mashed) and salt. Then the "wooden machine" will smash and mix it making a dough. Separate into small portions of the same size and this is it.

To sell, wrap it in banana leaf so it doesn't dry and get very hard (add a little oil to banana leaf so it doesn't stick).

The most popular and tasty ways of having it are fried or barbequed, although you can also eat it raw. It is usually eaten in winter and served with brown sugar or jaggery on the side. It only costs between 100-200 kyats ($0.1 - 0.2).

JAGGERY—TODDY PALM SYRUP

Jaggery is a traditional sugar made from date, cane juice or palm sap. In Myanmar, you can find it mostly around Bagan and it comes from toddy palm syrup. Locals climb to the top of the palm, cut a palm shoot and place a pot underneath to collect the white syrup.

The syrup collected before the morning can be used as a very refreshing and sweet drink. The one collected in the evening is already fermented, becoming sour and an alcoholic beverage.

To make jaggery, they simply boil this syrup until it becomes brown. Mixing jaggery and coconut makes a very good snack.

It is used a lot in Burmese kitchens as an ingredient to balance the heat of the spice, add colour and enrich the food.

In a restaurant or teashop it is always served as a snack after your traditional Burmese meal. A cup of green tea and jaggery is a perfect way to end your meal.

NOODLE MIX SALAD—STREET STALL

Daw Than Mya has one of the most traditional street food stalls in Myanmar, where she sells Noodle Mix Salad. This type of street stall has different kinds of noodles and a variety of ingredients such as tofu, lemon, cabbage, tomatoes, green papaya, crispy split-peas and many others.

This is a cold dish mixed by hand - you simply choose the noodles and ingredients you want in your mix and then add different spices and sauces to add flavour.

There's a choice of rice and flour noodles, and sauces and spices include dry chilli, bean powder, salt, tamarind sauce, fish thick sauce, oil with fried garlic and onion and tomato sauce with chilli.

A great snack anytime throughout the day, it's always accompanied by a soup, in this case, Daw Than Mya gives you Mohinga soup, since she also sells Mohinga (Myanmar National Dish, see page 24) in her stall.

J U A N   G A L L A R D O

NEED ECO VILLAGE FOUNDATION IN MYANMAR

NEED stands for Network for Environmental and Economic Development and is a not-for-profit organization that started seven years ago in Chiang Mai (Thailand) and is now expanding to Myanmar.

Khaing Dhu Wan is the founder and executive director and each year a group of students will enrol in this 10-month program to learn through nature, become community leaders and receive training on Land, Law & Economics.

NEED's main goals are the promotion of environmental conservation, sustainable agricultural and economic development in Myanmar. The students have been working on different ideas to implement in their own villages once they finish the training.

Cooking is another of the daily group activities. They use the organic vegetables that they grow and supplement this with produce that they buy from neighbouring farms, contributing also to the community development. It's amazing to see them cooking on a fire in the traditional way. It's always fun to share a table with them!

When I was there they cooked a lot of different dishes for me, but I'll show you just two of them: Mohinga and hot & spicy gourd and tomato dish.

Johanna teaches English and students love her. They were a little shy when I first met them but their confidence grew and they soon enjoyed practising their English with a foreigner. They are very curious to know about your personal life and the cultural differences between Myanmar and other countries.

JUAN GALLARDO

MOHINGA

Mohinga is Myanmar's National Dish and is featured on the cover of *Delicious Myanmar*.

It is a fish broth noodle soup typically consumed for breakfast, although you can buy it from street stalls and teahouses at any time of the day.

This dish is traditionally made with catfish and thin rice noodles.

NEED students cooked it and it was amazing! This is how they did it:

1. Boil fish with lemon grass and ginger. Then debone fish.
2. Mix gram flour with water to make a paste.
3. Cut the banana stem and boil them in water with onions, gram flour paste and add fish sauce.
4. Make the Myanmar spice sauce with: ginger (from cooking the fish), garlic, onion, cooking oil (peanut oil or sunflower oil), dried red chilli, turmeric, paprika. (See page 26)
5. Mix and heat fish meat with Myanmar spice sauce and gram flour paste.
6. Put together the previous mix with the banana stem and onions in boiling water. Ready!

How to serve: Put noodles in a bowl and add, as you like, boiled egg, coriander leaf, fried onions, fried garlic, lime juice, fish sauce, chilli powder and crispy split peas. Then pour soup until noodles are covered. Enjoy!

MYANMAR SPICE SAUCE

1. Dried Red Chilli
2. Onions
3. Garlic
4. Ginger
5. Turmeric Powder
6. Paprika
7. Cooking Oil (try Peanut oil or Sunflower oil)

Use a mortar and pestle to make the sauce with chilli, paprika, onions, garlic and ginger.

Then fry the mix in hot cooking oil in a wok and add turmeric powder in the mixture.

This is a base sauce used to spice up most Burmese dishes, like this hot and spicy gourd and tomato dish.

For a richer flavour you can just add fish sauce and if you want a great soup, add some boiling water.

CHINLON

Chinlon is a traditional game in Myanmar in which a woven rattan ball is kicked around. Informally, players form a circle anywhere they find a space and keep the ball as long as possible in the air by using the feet and any part of the body (head, shoulder, knee, heel, sole, chest...) except hands.

Usually there is no scoring and it's just for fun.

Another variation, this time with points and two teams of three players each, is played with a volleyball net and has a similar scoring system to volleyball. Only the head, feet and legs are allowed to touch the ball.

It's amazing to see the acrobatic jumps achieved to hit the ball!

Players usually play without shoes and if they are wearing longyi (traditional wrap around skirt for men), they tuck it up.

PHYO

Phyo is 26-years-old and originally from the Rakhine tribe. She lives in Yangon with her husband Meju and their 5-year-old daughter, Ju-One. It's a house of artists, she is a singer and Meju teaches guitar.

Phyo loves cooking and always volunteers to cook in group activities for the events at the Christian church she attends every weekend.

She always wears thanaka make-up, which is a cream used in Myanmar not only for cosmetic purposes, but also to protect the skin from the sun. (See page 42)

One of her dreams is to open a restaurant.

VERMICELLI SOUP WITH CHICKEN

This is a delicious noodle soup – although it might look a little crowded because of its many different ingredients. While Phyo prepared it, Meju joked that the dry mushrooms they use are called "mouse ears" because of the similar look.

1. In a big pot, boil water and add dry mushrooms.
2. With a mortar, mix ginger, onion, garlic and lime and add it to a pan with vegetable or peanut oil.
3. Add the chicken to the pan with the mix. The chicken has been previously seasoned with paprika, chicken powder, pepper and a little bit of turmeric powder.
4. Boil clear rice vermicelli.
5. Cut the fish cakes into small pieces.
6. Add the chicken, vermicelli and fish cake to the big pot of dry mushrooms.

Add some shrimp sauce and more chicken powder or paprika if needed.

Stir well and enjoy!

JUAN GALLARDO

WATERCRESS SALAD

Salads are very popular in Myanmar and this one is a favourite with the locals!

It's a mix of boiled watercress with fish paste, green chilli, chicken powder, lime, onion and garlic.
So simple, so good!

FISH BALLS WITH TOMATO

This is one of my favourite dishes. Colourful, delicious, beautiful!

1. Mix fish meat and red chilli powder and make balls to boil.
2. Boil tomatoes and peel off skin.
3. Heat vegetable oil in a wok and put together the tomatoes and fish balls.
4. Add green chilli.
5. Add fish paste, chicken powder, dry shrimp powder and salt.
6. Add onions and garlic.
7. Add coriander.

It's like a fish balls curry based on tomato sauce that gives to this dish a unique touch.

FISH CURRY

This fish curry is very tasty and goes perfectly with vegetables like drumsticks, which are very similar to ladies fingers but actually tastes really different.

1. First you have to season the fish pieces with salt, turmeric, paprika, chicken powder and dry shrimp powder.
2. Add a sauce made of water with ripe tamarind and fish paste.
3. Put everything in a pan with vegetable oil and add drumsticks and onions. You can also add some chilli if you want it spicy.

SHWE YIN AYE

Shwe Yin Aye is one of the popular and traditional desserts in Myanmar.

It's a combination of sticky rice, boiled sago, agar jelly, coconut milk, coconut, bread, sugar, green colour rice flour jelly and ice.

You can find small street stalls selling it everywhere in Myanmar. They usually have every ingredient already in a bowl or big glass and when you order it, then they just add the coconut milk. It's sweet, creamy and refreshing.

THANAKA

As you have already seen with Phyo, thanaka is the make-up of Myanmar. Thanaka wood comes from the Murraya tree and the cream is made by grinding the bark with a little water on a circular stone called kyauk pyin.

They apply the cream to their faces in a variety of ways, but common designs include circles or squares on the cheeks.

Another common design is achieved by using a brush. You apply the thanaka cream with your finger and afterwards you "brush it" to leave a trail.

Most women and children wear it in Myanmar not only for cosmetic reasons, but also to protect their skin from the sun and to provide a cooling effect. For this reason some men wear it too.

BEENA SHAH

Beena is an amazing artist who loves cooking. She moved to Yangon with her husband in 2002 and in 2010 she started teaching art and cookery.

Her classes are held in her beautiful apartment located at Shwegondaing Junction with spectacular views of the Shwedagon Pagoda.

Art classes are daily but the cookery ones are usually twice a week, on a flexible schedule. She is very patient and loves to teach.

The students who attend the cookery classes vary in ages and backgrounds, from local restaurant owners, to expats and tourists.

The cookery classes focuses on Indian cuisine, which has a big influence in Burmese dishes. You will learn how to cook a six-course set menu with a starter, soup, salad, entree, bread and a dessert. And yes, later you can eat it!

It's such a memorable moment to cook and later enjoy the meal together, all with Shwedagon Pagoda views.

PANEER MAKHANI

This is a very simple dish to prepare and so rich in flavours and spices. It uses paneer (unsalted white cheese) as the main ingredient.

First, you heat oil in a pan and add onion paste, cashew nut paste and chilli-garlic-ginger paste. Then you add the tomato paste and allow it to boil.

Now it's time to add a little bit of salt and all the different spices, which are cumin seed powder, garam masala, turmeric powder, red chilli powder and kasoori methi.

And finally, you add the cream, green peas and the paneer cubes. Let it boil and garnish it with coriander leaves before serving. Yum!

MIX DAL MAKHANI

Mix Dal Makhani is a very popular Indian curry made with a mix of dal (Indian lentils) and a blend of aromatic spices. This is the perfect dish to enjoy with paratha (Indian flat bread similar to naan), specially the one with garlic, my favourite! Beena teaches you how to make your own.

To prepare the mix for Dal Makhani you have to soak the dal for an hour and then boil them. Then in a separate pan, heat a little bit of oil and add cumin seeds, mustard seeds, green/red chillies and curry leaves. After a few minutes add onion, ginger paste and garlic.

Once this is well cooked, you can add all the spices, including red chilli powder, turmeric powder, coriander seeds powder, gram masala and salt.

When everything is well mixed, add the boiled dal and some cream, stir well and garnish with chopped coriander leaves.

Serve hot and get ready to dip the paratha.

SHWEDAGON PAGODA

Shwedagon Pagoda shimmers above the city of Yangon and it's pure beauty.

It has been sitting on Sanguttara Hill since 600 BC and it holds relics of the past four Buddhas. The pagoda has suffered wars, neglect and earthquakes but it is in excellent condition after restorations.

Before visiting it you will probably have seen it from a distance but you will never imagine how magical it is.

The golden stupa is gilded with gold leaves and the upper section is sheathed by pure gold plates, with the crowning umbrella studded with a variety of 83,850 items of jewellery. The umbrella weighs five tons (half a ton is of gold) and has 4,016 small gold bells. Above the umbrella there is the vane and on top of it at the highest point there is the diamond orb with 4,351 diamonds.

No matter how many times you see it, it always takes your breath away.

My recommendation is to go very early for the sunrise. It is especially beautiful in the morning with the light change and the moon disappearing. Also, at this time there are many worshippers and many different praying activities in the different shrines around the main pagoda. It's an absolute must-see in Yangon.

Don't visit it in a rush, enjoy its peaceful atmosphere and relax while so many local pilgrims give offerings, light candles and pray.

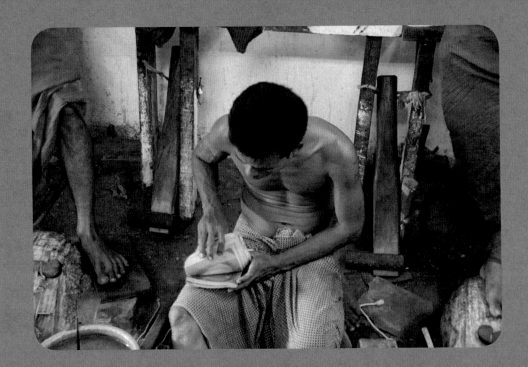

GOLD POUNDERS WORKSHOP, MANDALAY

Gold pounders workshops are popular in Mandalay and it's where they strike the gold to make it paper-thin.

It is manual labour at its extreme. The hammer itself weighs about 3kg and workers often suffer from bad backs after about 10 years of work.

The watch that tells gold pounders when to stop for a break is a coconut shell placed in a pot with water. The shell has a small hole in it and it takes one hour to fill up and sink. This is when they get a 15 minute break.

In another room in the workshops, there are women who receive the stacks of gold leaves that have been pounded and prepare the packages that are later sold to cover Buddha images in temples.

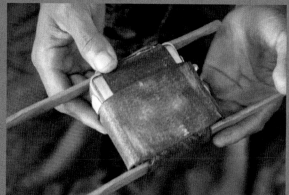

U BEIN BRIDGE

Located in the former capital city of Amarapura – just 10 km from Mandalay – U Bein Bridge is sure to be one of the highlights of your visit to Mandalay.

It is the longest teak bridge in the world, measuring 1.2 km and crossing Taungthaman Lake.

The teak wood, including the columns used as the bridge pillars, came from the royal palace at Amarapura. When the capital was moved to Mandalay they took it down and U Bein, the mayor, used the teak to build this bridge so locals could cross Taungthaman Lake. Only a few of the thousand old teakwood posts have been replaced with concrete, the majority remain intact.

During the day the bridge is very busy. It forms part of daily life as hundreds of locals cross it to get to and from work, kids to travel to school and back, monks to visit the monastery, ice cream vendors... From the little cafes on both sides of the lake, you can spend hours people watching!

There are also traditional boats that cross the lake from where you can get a close up view of the bridge.

In the hot season there is land around the lake that farmers make the most of before the rainy season floods the area.

Other must-sees near Mandalay are Inwa (or Ava), Mingun and Sagaing.

JUAN GALLARDO

INWA (OR AVA)

Inwa, like Amarapura, is located close to Mandalay. Combine these two beautiful and historical cities for the perfect day trip.

Inwa was the capital city of Burma for almost 360 years at five separate times between 1365 and 1842.

The most beautiful sight is Bagaya Monastery, a monastic college where the royals were educated. This Buddhist monastery was built in 1593 with 267 huge teak wood posts. Unfortunately it caught on fire in 1821 and the government reconstructed it and built a new brick building in place of the old monastery.

The monastery is decorated with amazing Burmese carvings and surrounded by nature, mainly palms and banana trees.

I suggest you visit Amarapura to watch the sunrise from U Bein Bridge and then spend the rest of the day in Inwa.

MINGUN

Mingun is in the Sagaing region, just crossing the Irrawaddy river and about 10 km from Mandalay which makes it another perfect day trip.

The attraction in Mingun is Pahtodawgyi, the remaining ruins of a massive stupa that King Bodawpaya began to build in 1790 using mostly slave labour.

It was intentionally left unfinished because the king was so superstitious. During the construction it was prophesied that the completion of the massive stupa would cause the destruction of the country.

Construction was slowed down to prevent the prophecy being fulfilled and when he died, the project was abandoned.

The pagoda as it is now is only 50 meters high, one third of the intended height, and has giant cracks from the earthquake in 1839.

What was finished was the bell, the largest bell in the world today with an outer diameter of 4.95 meters and a height of 3.66 meters. It weighs 55,555 viss (Burmese unit of measurement) (90 tons) with the inscription (၅), as well as a mnemonic "Min Hpyu Hman Hman Pyaw", with the consonants representing the number 5 in Burmese astronomy and numerology.

Funny fact is that it holds the world record for the largest pile of bricks!

DELICIOUS MYANMAR

COCONUT NOODLES

This flat wheat noodle dish with a creamy, light curry flavour is, after Mohinga, the most popular in Myanmar. It is also traditionally eaten in the morning and usually cooked for festivals and celebrations.

On this occasion, my friend Tina invited me to a Buddhist festival in her neighbourhood to see her mom and neighbours volunteering to cook the coconut noodles as a donation to the festival.

1. For the chicken, they fry the onions, garlic and ginger in a pan with oil before adding chilli powder and turmeric powder. Next the boneless chicken with some salt and chicken powder seasoning is added. The smell at this point is wonderful!
2. To prepare the coconut cream they boil water and add raw bean powder dissolved in water. Then they add coconut milk, salt, chicken powder, fish sauce and sugar. When everything is well mixed, the cooked chicken is added.
3. To serve, put the noodles in a bowl, add a hard boiled duck egg, rice crackers, raw onions and the coconut cream. Delicious!

For those who want to add even more flavour, it goes perfectly with chilli and/or lime.

SAING OO

Saing Oo is 31-years-old and lives happily in Pang Kam with her husband, their 8-year-old daughter and 6-year-old son.

Pang Kam is a small Padaung ethnic group village in the mountains near Hsipaw, in Shan State.

There are guides who organise trekking to the villages in the mountains from Hsipaw and Saing Oo always welcomes foreigners to stay overnight in her house.

She learned English at school between the ages of seven and fifteen. Now she relishes being able to practise her English with foreigners.

Saing Oo is always smiling and loves to cook the recipes she learned from her mum, Me Kan Yo and her auntie, Nai Yum.

Me Kan Yo

Nai Yum

POTATO, EGG AND TOMATO CURRY

This is one of the simplest curries imaginable. You can prepare it in just three steps and it's a great side dish to accompany your main. Check out the kitchen and wood fire cooker – I love it!

1. Boil the potatoes and the eggs.
2. Blend the tomatoes and add turmeric powder, salt and sugar.
3. Finally heat the oil and add onions. Then add the tomato mix that was previously prepared. When everything is well mixed, add the potatoes and eggs.

TEALEAF SALAD

This is a classic dish in Myanmar and you won't find it in many other countries!

Every single teahouse and restaurant will have it on the menu and it's also very common to have as a snack.

A mixture of pickled tealeaf, cabbage, onion, tomatoes, fried garlic, oil, salt, lime, there's also a mix of beans and nuts (fried beans, sesame seeds, peanuts...). You can even add dried shrimp if you want.

The tealeaf is pickled for one to two months with salt, oil and lime.

The salad has a very strong flavour and it's a dish to share while drinking green tea or as part of a traditional Burmese meal with many different dishes. The mixture of flavours and sensations are drawn from the variety of ingredients and cooking methods. It is definitely a culinary experience worth trying!

PAPAYA CURRY

Easy, delicious and healthy!

1. Slice raw, green papaya and clean it with water.
2. Heat oil, fry garlic and add salt, tomatoes and turmeric powder.
3. Add the papaya and wait until it has absorbed the curry and it's soft.

Serve with white rice and you've got a Burmese curry!

PUMPKIN CURRY

If you thought papaya curry was easy, this one is the winner.

1. Cut pumpkin in pieces.
2. Heat oil in wok and add turmeric powder and salt.
3. Add the pumpkin, boiling water and cover for 15-20 minutes.
4. At the end add some sugar and mix well.

It's sweet, colourful and tasty! Who would ever have thought of making a curry with pumpkin?

JUAN GALLARDO

STICKY RICE AND MUSIC

A curious fact about Myanmar food and culture is that sticky rice is used to tune drums, which also makes the drums more comfortable to play. They put the rice in the middle of the ox-skin surface of the drum as these photos at a festival in Pang Kam village shows.

JUAN GALLARDO

GOKTEIK VIADUCT, FROM PYIN OO LWIN TO HSIPAW

One of the most interesting and adventurous ways to get to Hsipaw is by train from Pyin Oo Lwin. You will cross the Gokteik Viaduct, which has amazing views but is also pretty scary. It was constructed in 1901 and is 97 meters in height and 688 meters in length. The scary part is when the train stops just before the bridge and then crosses it really slowly to prevent stress on the structure while you can hear it creaking…

JUAN GALLARDO

Pyin Oo Lwin is a small town with a very different atmosphere to other Myanmar towns. Founded by the British in 1896, it still has colonial buildings and people using horse carts. Most of the population are descendants of Indian and Nepali workers who came here to build the rail line. It has a botanical garden, National Kandawgyi Garden, which is a must-see.

J U A N   G A L L A R D O

Hsipaw is the perfect destination for hill-tribe treks, like Pang Kam village. It has a relaxed atmosphere, an intriguing riverfront market with hill-villagers selling their goods, and an area with old temples known as Little Bagan.

SHWAN KU, PADAUNG ETHNIC GROUP VILLAGE

Another Padaung ethnic group village I visited was Shwan Ku, in Pan Pat region, just 20 miles from Loikaw, Kayah State. It's a small, rural village with just a few houses where people live off the land.

Most women from Padaung ethnic group have followed their traditional culture of wearing neck rings. Girls first start to wear brass neck coils at the age of five. Over the years the coil is replaced by a longer one with more turns. The neck itself is not lengthened, the weight of the brass pushes the collar bone down and compresses the rib cage. However the younger generation seem not to want to continue with this tradition.

Villagers in this region believe in spirits (nats). This is their religious site to pray and ask for good luck, prosperity and good weather. The posts represent sun, moon and earth.

All houses in the village are made of wood and bamboo. In the main room they all have corn hanging from the ceiling just above the fireplace. This is the corn they will plant and grow. The reason for placing them there is to prevent birds from eating the corn seeds once they plant them. The smoked corn seeds will not attract the birds.

STICKY RICE STUFFED IN BAMBOO

A Myanmar favourite, this is a traditional seasonal snack which vendors sell at every festival.

My friend Kyaw Kyaw took me in Hsipaw to see how Daw Kin Than cooked it to sell at a Buddhist festival.

The type of bamboo used is called Tinwa and it is cut so it has only one end closed. They use this kind of bamboo because it has a skin inside and when you peel it to eat, the skin sticks to the rice and it's tastier. The stuffing is made of rice, peanut and coconut.

1. Soak the rice in water overnight, boil peanuts, grate coconut and mix all three.
2. Fill the bamboo with 70% mix and 30% water. Close with a top made of coconut hair, straw or weed, but not too tightly. Place the bamboo vertically across the fire to bake and when it becomes black burnt, peel off the burnt part.
3. Put it back on the fire but this time on a lower heat so it cooks thoroughly. Peel off the burnt part once again until the bamboo skin is very thin.

To eat it, peel very slowly and little by little so the inside skin of the bamboo gets stacked to the rice.

It's a very good snack for the cold season but not so good for digestion in the hot weather.

BAMBOO BUDDHA MONASTERY

In Little Bagan just on the edge of Hsipaw, you can find a beautiful old teak monastery. Within the Bamboo Buddha Monastery, there is a lacquered Buddha made from bamboo strips. You can't see the bamboo now because it is all covered in layers of gold.

In this monastery novice monks and their leader monk showed me how they barbecue banana crackers and how they set the table with all the food donated by neighbours from the morning when they go to collect alms. I got hungry just looking at the colourful table!

JUAN GALLARDO

YIN YIN THAN

Yin Yin Than is my friend Wai Yan's mum who prepared for me a full Burmese meal with three salads, two main dishes and a soup.

I enjoyed the whole Myanmar meal experience, including sitting on the floor at a short round table and eating with my hands. Which is not easy! When you take the food, you have to position your hand in the shape of a spoon and with your thumb push the food to your mouth. It takes practise, even more than chopsticks.

Yin Yin Than lives in a pleasant apartment in Yangon with Wai Yan's family and loves taking care of and playing with Khant Zay-Yatu, her 1-year-old grandson.

SWEET CHICKEN CURRY WITH TOMATO

This is a simple curry in which you fry a paste made of ginger and garlic, then add the chicken (previously mixed with yellow curry powder) and a little bit of salt, chicken powder and Chinese sauce. When it's ready, just add onions and tomatoes. Perfect served with steamed rice!

The yellow curry powder is a mixture of many spices including cumin, coriander, turmeric, cayenne pepper, mustard seed and ginger.

The Chinese sauce is similar to soy sauce and used for flavour or as a thickener or as browning.

FISH PASTE WITH GREEN PEPPER

A colourful and delicious dish, this is not one you often get in a restaurant. It's a curry sauce made of ginger, garlic, onion, tomatoes and red curry powder, in which the green capsicum filled with fish paste is cooked.

JUAN GALLARDO

MARIAN FRUIT SALAD

This is a very popular salad and an easy one to find on street stalls.

Slice the green marian plum and mix with onions, dry prawn powder, fried onion and garlic, chicken powder, bean powder, coriander and smashed peanuts.

To mix it properly, heat a little bit of oil with turmeric powder and add it to the mix.

JUAN GALLARDO

FERMENTED SOYBEAN PASTE SALAD

You are mostly likely to find this paste in the Bagan area.

It's thick and powerful in flavour, and mixed with onion, garlic and oil. Although it doesn't look that appealing, as a side dish mixed with steamed rice, it'll really surprise you.

This is an example of Burmese cuisine that will definitely take you out of your comfort zone!

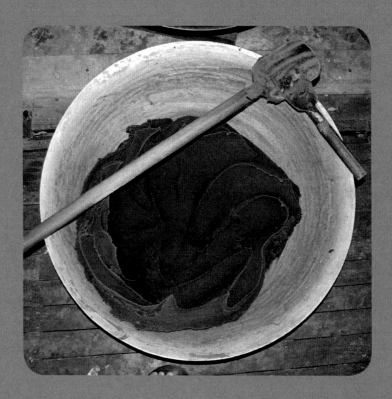

FERMENTED SOYBEAN PASTE WORKSHOP

This is a workshop in Nyaung U, Bagan, where my friend Ko Ko showed me how easy it is to make this paste.

The soybean is heated in water for three hours and then separated from the water. The coolest part of the process is that they recycle the beans to feed the horses and for the fire they don't use wood, instead they use the shells from peanuts.

The water is heated again and again during the three hour period for a total of two days, decreasing the fire intensity.

BAGAN

Bagan is a top attraction in Myanmar and guaranteed to be the highlight of your trip. Bagan Archaeological Zone has over 2,000 pagodas and with the Irrawaddy River flowing past, the scenery is magical.

Nyaung U is the busiest city in the area with lots of hotels and restaurants. To explore the most important temples you'll need a couple of days and most tourists either rent bicycles or hire horse carts for the day.

Bagan is not only about the temples, it is really easy and exciting to get lost exploring the rural villages of the area. You will often see farmers doing their daily rounds on their bullock cart and they are all extremely friendly.

Two of the most fascinating temples are Thatbyinnyu which stands out from the others because it is all white, and my favourite, Sulamani Temple.

In Bagan, you simply have to experience sunrise and sunset. Absolutely marvellous! There are famous temples with the best views but these are usually crowded. From my experience, you get a fantastic view from just about any temple. So find your favourite, relax, and enjoy!

BURMESE PARASOLS

The traditional Burmese parasol is handmade with cotton and bamboo strings.

The cotton is hand-painted with different designs and lacquered so that they can stand up to sunshine and rain. The main bamboo structure is sewed using an intricate pattern.

This is a workshop in Pathein, near Yangon, where you can see how they are made. In Yangon you can find them in Bogyoke market in many different sizes, from tiny for decoration to three meters in diameter for the garden.

You usually see monks and nuns walking in the streets of Myanmar with them as protection from the sun or rain.

BAMBOO HAT

These typical Burmese hats are handmade from bamboo husks in workshops like this one on Ogre Island, Mawlamyine, Moulmein.

The bamboo husk comes from very thick bamboo canes and is cut to form the pattern. They are then joined together using thin bamboo strings and finally the rims are edged with bamboo strings and sewn with a strong thread.

Funny fact: The peak at the top of the hat on the left is made from a piece of plastic from an old bag of potato chips!

MOE ZAW, PARADISE RESTAURANT, NGAPALI BEACH

Moe Zaw was born in Chaung Tha and moved to Pathein when he was 10-years-old. In 2000 he went to Ngapali and worked as a waiter in two different restaurants over six years. He then ran his own restaurant for four years but had to sell it and return to Pathein because of his father's ailing health. After two years back in Pathein, in 2012 he returned to Ngapali to open Paradise restaurant.

Every morning he goes to the beach and nearby hotels to meet people and tell them about his restaurant. While he runs the restaurant, his brother-in-law Zaw Zaw Aung, helps him as a waiter and with shopping for fresh food in the market. His wife Thida San, sister-in-law Thida Win and Aye Myint cook all the delicious food for the restaurant.

Let's see a few of their fresh seafood dishes. Yum!

CHILLI CRAB

This is one of my favourite seafood dishes, so spicy it numbs your lips but you still can't stop eating.

To cook, heat oil in a pot and add chilli, onion, garlic, turmeric powder, salt, oil, chicken powder and fish sauce or soya sauce (optional). When it's hot and mixed, add the crab. Cook for approximately 10 minutes.

It's delicious with steamed rice to soothe the heat. My favourite drink to go with this is green tea.

FISH IN BANANA LEAF

I love this one.

Aye Myint picked a banana leaf from his garden, cleaned it with water and then dried it in the fire.

Meanwhile, Thida Win cut the fish into thick filets and mixed in a bowl onions, tomatoes, coconut powder, salt, pepper and chicken powder.

She cut the leaf in smaller pieces, spread butter on it, put the fish on top of the butter and added the previous mix on top of the fish with some extra coconut powder and pepper on top.

Wrap it, steam it for 10 minutes and enjoy!

I really liked it with steamed rice and an avocado salad on the side.

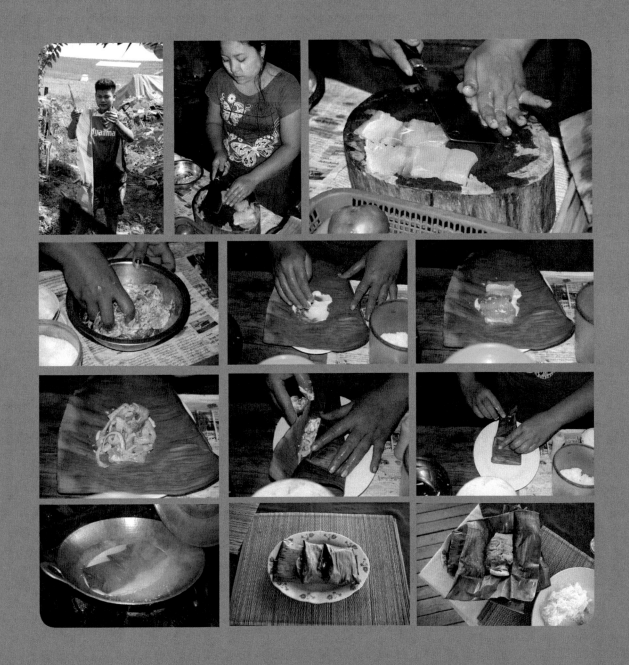

TIGER PRAWN CURRY

Myanmar curries are truly delicious and this one with king prawns always reminds me of Ngapali beach!

The curry sauce is made with tomatoes, onions, chicken powder, salt, turmeric, chilli powder, soy sauce and curry powder or pepper.

To prepare it, blend tomatoes and onions and heat it in a pot. Then add chilli powder and soy sauce. Finally add prawns (or the seafood of your choice) previously seasoned with salt, chicken powder and turmeric. Sprinkle curry or pepper at the end.

After a hard day of work in Ngapali beach planning the best walk, eating exotic fruits, sunbathing, swimming in crystal clear water, words can't even begin to describe how good this dish is for dinner.

RAKHINE FISH CURRY

This curry is from Rakhine State and it's not on the menu. Thida Win cooked it for me after I tried and loved it when they had it one lunch-time.

It's very spicy and goes well with vegetables, meat or fish.

For this dish you need fresh tamarind, fish paste, green chilli, salt and chicken powder.

To prepare the tamarind sauce, put the tamarind in a little bowl and add hot water. Dissolve and mix well. Remember to remove the tamarind seeds.

For the fish paste, prepare a sauce mixing it with boiling water too.

And for the chillies, just boil them in water to make them softer, then crush them.

Put everything together in a pot and add water, the vegetables and diced meat or fish.

If you like spicy and rich flavour, this is your curry!

JUAN GALLARDO

NGAPALI BEACH

Ngapali beach is the most popular tourist beach in Myanmar. Although it's a long trip by bus because of the road conditions, it has an airport which makes it really easy to escape from busy Yangon.

Located in the Bay of Bengal in Rakhine State, its white sand, clear blue waters and lined up palm trees will make you want to stay there forever.

What I love about Ngapali is that as you step outside the beach, you are surrounded by the rural community. You can walk to the local market, teahouse, monastery and be amazed by the beautiful traditional houses built with wood and bamboo and surrounded by palm trees.

In the morning, you can see women on the beach spreading out fish on nets to dry in the sun and in the evening, treat your eyes and soul to one of the best sunsets.

Perfect place to relax and finish your trip!

NGWE SAUNG BEACH

Ngwe Saung beach is a five hour drive from Yangon. It is known for its twin rock stupas and is an unspoilt 15km long beach with fine white sand and clear blue sea.

The sunset here is marvellous!

INLE LAKE

A boat trip around Inle lake is a must-do in Myanmar.

As well as fishermen, you will see their floating villages and floating gardens.

The houses are made of bamboo and sit on top of long bamboo canes that hold them above the lake. The space under their houses is used to store their boats, as well as do the laundry.

The villagers who live in these huts have developed a unique way to power their boats. They pedal with their feet, leaving their hands free for other things such as pulling up fishing nets or harvesting tomatoes.

The reason they do this is because there are many reeds and water plants in the lake, and if they row sitting down in the boat they can't see them. Standing on the end of the boat they have a great view and can lead the way better.

The fishing boats are traditionally carved from teak and the fishing method rather unusual. Cone-shaped nets are made from bamboo or cane, with a small net inside that is opened at the top.

They put their boats together and put the cone-shaped net into the water, then press on it with their feet so it sinks to the bottom where the fish are, and finally with the cone sunk and the fish trapped, they spear from above through the opening at the top of the cone.

They can use this method because the lake is not very deep, in the dry season the average water depth is only about two meters.

The surrounding mountains form a dramatic backdrop to this stunning lake and if you rent a bicycle and explore a little bit around the lake you will see authentic Myanmar rural life.

YUUKA AND LUN MON

My friend Yuuka is 32-years-old and invited me to Naung Ping, a little village in Shan State where she grew up and where her family still lives. For the past six years, Yuuka has lived in Malaysia. She likes cooking (especially Thai and Japanese), travelling and singing.

Taw Aye Un is Yuuka's mom and very respected in her neighbourhood. She is a sort of village counsellor, helping young couples and people in the village to resolve their arguments. She also helps villagers to buy tickets for travelling and is the leader of the women's drum band in festivals.

Lun Mon is Yuuka's friend and neighbour. He is a corn and sugar cane farmer and likes cooking and organizing all the events in the neighbourhood – down to the last detail.

They cooked me a Shan State favourite - Shan Yellow Rice Cake with Tomato Sauce.

Taw Aye Un

SHAN YELLOW RICE CAKE WITH TOMATO SAUCE

This is one of the dishes I tried on my first visit to Myanmar. It stuck with me and I definitely had to include it in this book. It's quite filling but so good!

For cooking the rice there is no trick, just wash it, add water, turmeric powder for the yellow colour, salt and a little bit of chicken powder. Don't cook it too much, in fact leave it a little hard.

There are two different tomato sauces, one to mix with the rice and another one to put on top of the rice cake.

For the first one, cut tomatoes in half, add salt and cook them in a pot until you have a sauce. Leave to cool. Remove the tomato skin.

Then you stir the yellow rice to make it a little bit sticky and mix it with this tomato sauce.

Before pouring all the tomato sauce, separate some in a bowl and add turmeric oil. Use this mix to wet your hands and season the rice cake while you shape it.

The second tomato sauce to add on top of the cake is the key. To prepare it, heat oil and add onions, garlic, fermented soya bean powder, dried chilli powder and turmeric powder. Then add grained tomatoes, salt and chicken powder.

At this point you can also add coriander or spring onion and chicken or pork.

There is always another side sauce to add on top of the cake, turmeric and garlic sauce. Just heat oil, fry garlic and then add turmeric powder. I love this crunchy-garlic touch!

Any cracker like pork skin, bean or rice goes perfectly with this dish.

JUAN GALLARDO

RICE FIELDS AND CAVES IN PHA-AN (KAREN STATE)

Myanmar is an agricultural country where the rice industry is extremely important not only for exporting, but also as food security. According to government statistics, Myanmar has the world's highest annual rice consumption.

The colours in the paddy fields are amazing! The contrast of bright and vibrant green against the more yellow, dryer rice plants make for picture-perfect shots.

Here in Pha-an I had one of my most memorable experiences riding on a teak canoe across the paddy fields. It was a peaceful and quiet ride surrounded by nature, but risky, since one false move in the canoe to take a photo could land you in the water!

My ride started in Saddar cave, a beautiful place full of Buddha images. You can walk all the way through to the other side of the mountain and there you can ride the canoe back to the entrance of the cave across the paddy fields. Impressive!

JUAN GALLARDO

KYAUK KALAP PAGODA

After Saddar cave you can visit Kyauk Kalap pagoda, which is set near Pha-an in a privileged location in the middle of an artificial lake and on top of a sheer rock. From here there are spectacular views of Mount Zwegabin, especially during the sunset.

AMY TAO

Amy is very entrepreneurial and knows everybody in Bogyoke Market (Scott market) in Yangon. She sells Burmese cloth to shops and exports to Thailand.

She also has an internet router in her house and charges neighbours a discount rate for using it. As internet service in Myanmar is really expensive, she came up with this great idea to share costs.

Having once lived in Germany herself, she has many international friends living in Yangon to whom she teaches Burmese in the evenings after work. Amy loves food and laughingly told me that her friends always bribe her with food in order to convince her to go out with them.

MEAT BALLS AND TOMATO SALAD

For the mix, Amy uses minced beef, eggs, chopped onions, salt, chicken powder and mint. You can also add some red chilli to spice it up!

An alternative way to do the meatballs is to make a soup with water, garlic, salt and coriander and cook smaller size balls in it.

Amy prepared one of the most popular salads in Myanmar – tomato salad or as they called it, tomato mix – to serve with it. The ingredients are tomatoes, onions, green chilli and coriander.

JUAN GALLARDO

GRACEWORKS, YANGON

Myint Zu, Sarah and Naw Zu Zu are three young trainees recruited for Graceworks in Yangon.

Graceworks is a free training and employment initiative for disadvantaged youth in Myanmar and one of the activities they do to fund this program is cooking classes.

All three come from different parts of the country and joined this 10-month course that will provide them with food handling and kitchen management skills, English and computer training as well as personal development and life skills education.

These young students love to take foreigners to the market to buy ingredients, explain how to use them and teach how to cook several authentic dishes with them.

LOCAL MARKETS

Something I love to do in every new city I visit in Myanmar is to go to the local market. There are usually different ones at different times, ranging from the really early morning ones to the night ones.

The markets are very popular and always busy. If you are a curious person, it's a lot of fun to interact with the local vendors, who are always happy to explain how to cook something and give you a sample to try.

Normally the early morning markets have fish and seafood which comes straight from the harbour and also vegetables from nearby farmers who come to the city to sell their crops.

At night time when the heat has dropped, it's time for the meat and more fish and seafood.

During the day stalls are very colourful with exotic fruits and vegetables and at night they are very mysterious with lights and candles adding to the atmosphere.

JUAN GALLARDO

Vendors often face the dilemma whether to offer products like meat and seafood to tourists who can't cook them in their hotels. After giving it some thought, this woman finally decides with a lovely and shy smile to offer me the fish.

DELICIOUS MYANMAR

JUAN GALLARDO

HIN HTOTE

My friend Wai Yan took me to a family-run teahouse in Loikaw where they prepare the famous Hin Htote – a mixture of rice, spring onions and pork – all wrapped in banana leaf and steamed.

Spice it up with chilli sauce and enjoy with a piece of this root (Juu). Each bite is deliciously refreshing!

WUT YEE

Wut Yee is a food writer and contributing editor of Food Magazine. Her first book about international food (written in Burmese) was published last year and has been very successful.

She trained at the International Culinary Course in 2008 at Star Resources Hospitality & Training Center and has also been inspired by other cookbooks and even the internet.

She loves cooking and her favourite dish is Kachin Chicken Curry. I was delighted when she invited me to her house to cook this dish.

In her blog she has over 200 recipes from all over the world written in Burmese and also English.

Here are a few questions I asked her about Myanmar cuisine:

1. How would you describe Myanmar cuisine?

    Our cuisine is very rich in flavour and we use some unique cooking ingredients like chilli oil, flour and fish paste.

2. What do you like the most about Myanmar cuisine?

    I like a lot of the popular dishes like Noodle with Fish Soup (Mohinga), Pork Curry with Pone-Yay-Gyi, Fish Rice Cake (Shan style), Shan Noodles and Coconut Noodles.

3. What are the most common flavours?

    Oily and spicy – but in a good way. We often use bean powder, chilli powder and fish paste (nga pi) to absorb these flavours and enrich the taste.

4. Is Myanmar cuisine a good option for vegetarians?

   Yes. We have a lot of vegetarian recipes because we eat more vegetables than meat at a typical meal.

5. Is the food similar to that of the neighbouring countries?

   We are surrounded by big nations like China and India which are famous for their great cuisine. We do borrow some elements from both countries and that creates a hearty blend of cuisines unique to Myanmar.

6. Describe a traditional family meal. How many dishes are there?

   Vegetables, boiled, pickled or raw, and eaten with fish sauce is essential in a traditional family meal. We have a main meal, a salad and soup. All of these dishes are usually served with rice.

7. What's your favourite meal?

   My favourite meal is Chicken Ka Chin Chat or Kachin Chicken Curry which is a famous indigenous dish. The chicken is cooked with praew leaves. Some recipes use bamboo shoot and the result is a nice blend of sour and spicy curry. It goes well with a bowl of white rice.

KACHIN CHICKEN CURRY

Wut Yee taught me how to cook this dish and she's right, it's a tasty sour and spicy curry you'll love!

1. Marinate the chicken with garlic, ginger, turmeric, salt and chicken powder. Then mix together in a bowl minced coriander, basil, chillies and praew leaves or Vietnamese coriander.
2. Soak the dry chin saw char fruit in water for a while to get the juice. If you don't have this dry fruit, you can use lime juice instead.
3. Pour oil and chilli powder in a wok and fry the marinated chicken a bit.
4. Add the dry chin saw char juice, water, basil, Vietnamese coriander, chillies, coriander, salt and chicken powder, and let it boil until the chicken is cooked.
5. Add pickled bamboo shoots and keep it boiling a few more minutes adding more water if required.

Add some coriander leaves, basil and Vietnamese coriander for a final decorative touch. Serve with steamed rice and enjoy your meal!

Besides all the delicious dishes featured in this book, Myanmar also has a fascinating variety of street food, snacks and desserts to offer. Below are some of my favourites.

19TH STREET, YANGON

Well known for barbeques and drinks, this is a great place to hang with your friends for dinner or just drinks. You choose the barbeque stall you want to try, select your sticks and they'll cook them for you. Fish in the middle of the table to share while having drinks is very popular. Hope you've mastered using chopsticks by now!

My friend Sai loves to come here, hang out with his friends and make new friends with foreigners. One of his favourite snacks to go with beer is crickets. He'll even recommend a cricket for you, depending on how juicy you want it.

PORK HOT POT STALL

This is the most popular stall with locals. There are sticks around the hot pot with every cut of pork imaginable including the intestines, ear, tongue and more, which locals love dipping in a chili sauce.

If you're a pork lover who is not afraid to try new things, this is the stall for you.

FALOODA AND SUGAR CANE JUICE

I recommend you try Falooda and sugar cane juice, especially if you have a sweet tooth.

Falooda is made with a mixture of rose syrup, vermicelli or agar agar jelly, basil seeds, sago or tapioca pearls (white or coloured), ice-cream, milk or water, and pudding. Kids love to prepare falooda at home. It's cold, sweet and beautiful!

Sugar cane juice is perfect in the hot season. You really appreciate a stop in one of the stalls selling freshly-squeezed sugar cane juice. You'll notice them by the sound of bells.

E KYA KWAY

The king of snacks is E kya kway. It's made of fried dough and you can have it with sugar, dip in your tea or coffee, with yellow beans...as you like. The teahouses usually have them laid out on the tables and you just help yourself. Good luck trying to resist!

MYANMAR TEA

Tea in Myanmar is very sweet, made of condensed milk, black tea, whole milk and a little bit of boiling water. It is the official drink when you meet your friends in a teahouse. Yangon is the perfect place to enjoy a cup of tea in one of its many teahouses while mingling with the locals. I love it!

My friend Ko Win Zaw and his wife Ma Maw Maw Win have had this Street teahouse in the corner of Mahabandoola and 45th Street in Yangon for 15 years. Their only free day is Sundays and they use it to clean the house and visit pagodas.

He taught me the basic vocabulary to order in a teahouse which is always a great place to meet and chat with the locals.

JUAN GALLARDO

Made in the USA
Las Vegas, NV
10 November 2021